Birds of Prey

Birds of Prey

Emma Ford

B T BATSFORD LTD   LONDON

Frontispiece:
**The Changeable
Hawk Eagle**

ISBN 0 7134 4164 X

Filmset by Servis Filmsetting Ltd, Manchester
and printed in Hong Kong
for the publishers
B T Batsford Ltd
4 Fitzhardinge Street
London W1H 0AH

Contents

Acknowledgments

I would like to express my thanks to my husband, to Robert Boucher, to my Mother for typing the manuscript, and to Robert Hallmann for his beautiful photographs.

Preface

My purpose in writing this book is to provide an insight into the sport of falconry. However, the book is not intended as an instructional manual. Readers wishing to obtain a comprehensive handbook should refer to my larger work, *Falconry in Mews and Field*, Batsford, London, 1982. I hope, however, to reveal the substance of the sport, and thus to convey to those who are interested, and, more importantly, to those who are considering taking up the sport, a little of what falconry entails in the way of time and resources, and some of the pleasure to be derived from it.

Steppe Eagle

1 What is Falconry?

By definition, falconry is the art of taking wild quarry with a trained hawk. Most people are vaguely aware that falconry involves flying a trained bird at prey, but the way in which this is achieved remains something of a mystery. To unfold this mystery is to delve into the formation of a relationship between bird and man.

The first point to establish is that the bond between falconer and hawk is centred largely around food. Falconry was devised initially as a means of obtaining fresh meat. Thus the hawk was a food-provider for the falconer. Nowadays there are many reasons why people like to fly hawks, but gaining food does not figure particularly high on the list. However, the other side to the food relationship has not altered. A hawk will only respond to training if food is used as the incentive. It does not fly for the falconer for the same reasons as a dog works for its master — namely out of love, trust, loyalty and obedience, culminating in a desire to please. Nor can a hawk be reprimanded like a dog — by spoken word or remonstrative action. To induce a hawk to respond to training it is necessary to bring it into the same condition as would cause it to hunt in its natural state. This condition is controlled by the desire for food. A wild hawk will not kill needlessly — out of aggression or to satisfy a whim, because killing requires great exertion.

Therefore it only kills when it is hungry. The same is true of a falconry bird, but the focal point of the hunger is moved initially from the quarry to the falconer, for it is the falconer who offers food to the hawk in an attempt to call the bird to him. A fat bird would ignore the offer, but a bird which was sufficiently hungry would overcome its fear of the falconer in order to satisfy its hunger.

Thus the initial stage of falconry is the building up of a relationship between the falconer and his hawk in which the bird looks on man as a food-provider, and responds by coming to him for food. The second stage is to use the hawk's natural ability and instinct to kill, whilst still inducing it to work with the falconer.

It is a popular misconception that a hawk, once trained, will retrieve its kill to the falconer. In reality, having made a kill, the hawk has gained its food, and will break into the quarry and start to eat, continuing to do so until the falconer arrives on the scene to encourage the hawk from the kill with a reward of food held in his fist. The hawk can then be flown again at quarry if its hunger is not completely satisfied.

This is what falconry is all about — the control of the hawk's natural instincts and ability through training to work in partnership with man.

2 Equipment

The equipment or 'furniture' used whilst handling and training a bird of prey has remained virtually unchanged in both form and function since the earliest days of falconry. Much of the bird's equipment is made from leather, and this must be crafted by the falconer to fit his hawk. Some of the items are very difficult to make, but these can be easily obtained from equipment suppliers, who make and market equipment specifically for falconry.

Left:
Assorted equipment – from left to right: rabbit lure, creance, glove, variety of hoods, arm brace, falconry bag, and swing lure

Right:
Tawny Eagle in flight, showing jesses trailing behind

I will explain first the equipment which is used on the bird.

Jesses are attached to the legs of a hawk. These are leather straps of equal length fastened comfortably around the legs in such a way that they cannot tighten. They have several functions, the most important of which is to enable the falconer to retain the bird on the fist.

The jesses are attached to a swivel. This is made of metal. Its function is to prevent the jesses from becoming twisted. Normally one end of a swivel is larger than the other – the jesses are attached to the larger end, whilst a leash is put through the smaller end. The leash is used to tether the hawk when it is not being handled by the falconer. It is normally about 3ft in length. Traditional leashes, like the jesses, were made from leather, but nowadays we prefer to use braided nylon as this is stronger, and does not crack as leather will when wet.

Trained hawks usually have bells attached to their legs to enable the falconer to trace them when they are flying free. There are several types of bells which are designed especially for hawks – being lightweight but also of clear tone which can be heard over a good distance. The bells are sold in pairs, each bell of the pair having a different tone. Choice of two bells to make up a well-pitched pair depends upon the ear of the individual falconer. The bells are attached to a hawk's legs by means of leather straps called bewits, which are positioned above the jesses. Bells are often essential if a falconer is to find his bird when it has made a kill, and is sitting on quarry out of his sight. As the hawk uses its feet to kill its prey the bells will be heard. Some species of hawk have a habit of shaking their tails from side to side when they are sitting still. Such birds have bells attached to their tails. Others bob their heads, and consequently bells are put around their necks. In our age of advancing technology, some falconers are now using telemetry systems to trace their birds. The hawk is fitted with a small, lightweight radio-transmitter. This emits a signal which can be picked up over a restricted range by the falconer using an aerial and receiver.

Most people are familiar with the image of a hooded falcon. The function of a hood is to cover the hawk's eyes, excluding all light so that the bird is blindfolded. A hawk which cannot see will sit completely still and quiet. Hoods are used, therefore, whenever a falconer wishes to have his bird still and at ease. They are frequently used when travelling, or when it is necessary to perform some duty on the bird such as veterinary examination, or merely to fit new jesses. They are used when more than one bird is being taken hunting – the one which is not being flown remains hooded while the other one is shown the quarry by removal of the hood. Falcons are usually flown in a manner called 'flying out of hood'. This simply means that the falcon is hooded when carried out hunting. When quarry is sighted, the hood is removed and the falcon is put on the wing.

The falconer's furniture comprises several items, the most important of which is the glove. Falconry gloves must be strong enough to withstand the bird's talons, yet supple enough to enable the falconer to feel the jesses in the palm of his hand. A glove which extends an inch or so beyond the wrist will be sufficient for a small hawk, whilst for a larger bird, such as an eagle, a falconer needs a glove which extends to the elbow, to accommodate the span of such a bird's feet. Falconry gloves are usually worn on the left hand. Traditionally a falconer in mediaeval times used his left hand for his hawks in order to keep his sword-arm free. Falconers who rode on horseback while hunting with hawks would need their right hand to control their horse. Nowadays, the tradition has been maintained because it is practical for a right-handed person to keep their right hand free. For example, it is easier to tie the falconer's knot – used to tether hawks to their perches – with the right hand. Left-handed people usually carry hawks on their right hand

Peregrine falcon
being hooded

for the same reason.

All falconers must wear a bag when hawking, to hold the paraphernalia necessary to fly a hawk. There are many different designs of falconry bags, all of which have certain features in order to be functional. A bag has at least two compartments, placed back-to-back so that there is one on each side. It has a swivel at the top so that it can be turned easily from one side to the other with the free hand. The compartments are covered by flaps to prevent the hawk from peering inside to see the meat. Often bags have several other smaller compartments – to hold a spare swivel and leash, or to sheath a small knife used to cut up meat for the hawk. The bag is hung on the opposite side from the gloved hand, and is usually worn on a shoulder strap. A belt is then passed over the shoulder strap to hold the bag against the body, preventing it from bouncing as the falconer runs. The belt itself can incorporate certain useful features, such as a clip on which a glove can be hung when not in use. A block of wood carved to make a 'hood block' can be screwed to the belt, enabling the falconer to slip the hood over the block when it is removed from the bird, thus preventing the hood from becoming crushed in the bag or lost in the field.

When a falconer is training his hawk, a light line called a 'creance' is attached to its swivel. A creance consists of braided nylon line, of the type used for curtain cord. It is normally between 25 and 50 yards long, and is wound around a creance stick in a method best described as 'figure-of-eight' winding. This method can, by dint of much practice, be perfected with one hand, enabling the falconer to wind up his creance while his hawk is on the fist.

To train a hawk to hunt, a falconer uses a lure. Lures have food attached and resemble the prey which the bird is intended to hunt. Thus the bird associates the appearance of the quarry with the shape of the lure, and consequently will chase the prey. There are two principal types of lure – a rabbit lure and a swing lure. The former consists of a dried skin which is stretched around a piece of well-padded wood. A length of line, attached to one end, is used to drag the lure along the ground. The swing lure is designed to resemble a bird in flight, and is used for falcons who take their quarry in mid-air. Whenever possible, a falconer uses a fresh dead bird of the type the falcon is being trained to hunt, but because it is not always possible to have a daily supply of dead rooks, grouse, partridge etc, an artificial substitute must be made up. This consists of a pair of dried wings of the intended quarry, tied together, back to back. Meat is tied on to the wings, and a length of line – the 'lure line' – runs from the wings to the lure stick. The line is usually a length of braided cotton, because nylon line would burn and blister the falconer's fingers as he swung the lure.

When a hawk is not being handled or flown it is tethered to a perch. There are three main types of perch – the block, the bow and the ring.

The block perch is used for falcons, or 'longwings' because in their wild state falcons usually perch on a flat surface. It is made from a block of rounded and tapered wood, from which a metal stake protrudes from the thinner end. The stake has a metal ring around it on to which the falcon's leash is tied. The far end of the stake is sunk into the ground. The top of the block is usually covered with carpet, cork, or Astroturf.

The bow perch is designed for hawks, or 'shortwings', which perch in trees in their natural state, and are thus accustomed to gripping around a branch. The bows are made from a semi-circle of wood or padded metal, with a ground line of metal and points extending beyond the ground line to sink into the ground. The metal tethering ring passes freely over the top of the bow.

The ring perch is used as a substitute for the bow perch for 'shortwings'. It is a circle of metal – padded at the top for the hawk to sit on, with leather straps crossing the circle to prevent the hawk from bating through the middle. The circle is on a metal stem, on which the tethering ring is

Steve Ford with a Caracara on the gloved fist

16

Left:
**The Long-legged
Buzzard catching
the rabbit lure**

Right:
**African Steppe
Eagle on bow perch**

positioned, and the stem joins a ground line of metal on two stakes to sink into the ground.

There is a fourth variety of perch still unfortunately used by some falconers, called the screen perch. This perch is a straight wooden beam from which hessian is suspended. When on this perch a hawk cannot reach the ground. It is tied up against the swivel, and thus can only move within the length of the jesses. If the bird should bate off the screen perch, it can climb back up by using the hessian. However, if a hawk feels unwell and wants to lie down, it cannot reach the ground, but will hang upside down and die.

There are various other miscellaneous items which a falconer usually has among his equipment. A complete set of leather-working tools – knives, scalpels, waxed thread, hole punchers, rivets, eyelets etc – is obviously essential. A pot of grease is necessary to keep leather supple, and prevent it from cracking. For eagles, some falconers have arm braces to support the gloved hand, thus taking the weight off the arm. Identity tags, of the type used for dog collars, are sometimes put on hawks which are flying free. These are slipped on to a bewit with the aid of a small split ring. Falconers who cannot whistle their hawks with their mouths need a metal whistle, such as a shepherd's or referee's whistle, to call their birds.

Finally, one of the most important items of a falconer's furniture is a pair of scales. A hawk which is being trained must be weighed each day, for reasons which will be explained in the chapter on training. Balance scales of the old fashioned grocer's variety are the only type of weighing apparatus which can be used safely. The individual weights can then be adjusted when the bird is weighed to an accuracy of a quarter-of-an-ounce.

It is extremely important for any would-be-falconer to realize just how much equipment is necessary in order to practise falconry. It is essential to obtain the important items before obtaining a hawk.

White-bellied Sea Eagle

3 Daily Care

Broadwinged Hawk from America

There is a great deal more to keeping a bird of prey than simply flying it. To maintain a hawk to a high standard requires both good facilities and effort. I will first examine the facilities necessary to house a hawk.

Accommodation for a hawk can take many forms, according to the circumstances of the falconer. The hawk can be left day and night in a permanent outdoor shelter or 'weathering', as it is correctly called. This is constructed from three solid sides with a sloping roof to protect the hawk from the elements. The floor is covered in peat, sand, or gravel.

Alternatively a hawk can be housed in a 'mews', which is a light, airy, draught-proof and easily cleaned shed or building. Peat is put on the floor to soak up the 'mutes' or droppings. The mews is used only for night-time accommodation. During the day a hawk is put out to 'weather' on the 'weathering ground' or in a 'weathering'. A weathering ground is simply a level stretch of lawn where a hawk can be left on a perch or 'blocked' during the day, instead of being put into a weathering.

Accommodation for a hawk can be costly to construct. A shed to serve as a mews is expensive to buy, if the falconer does not have a suitable building. Even a weathering is costly to build from scratch, and even more expensive if it has to be protected by a complete wire netting surround from local dogs, cats, children, and the like.

In terms of daily care, a hawk is an intelligent, thinking being. It must not be shut up for days on end in a mews, seldom being put out to weather because its owner is too lazy or too busy. Nor will it appreciate being stuck away in a miserable little weathering, with nothing to see but the neighbour's fence opposite. Although a weathering should be positioned in a sheltered, draught proof spot, a hawk must be able to see some sort of activity from time to time, human or otherwise, to prevent it from becoming bored. Thus a hawk's accommodation must not only be well-designed, but also well-placed.

Every morning a hawk is put out to weather (unless it is already in a permanent outdoor weathering). Its equipment is checked for signs of wear, and its jesses are greased periodically to keep the leather supple. Most hawks like bathing, particularly in fine weather, so it is necessary to position a bath close to the bird's perch. The mews and weathering are raked over daily, and the mutes are checked for healthiness. Hawks will regurgitate pellets or 'castings' after eating roughage – fur or feathers. The castings are formed from the roughage, which must be fed to the bird two or three times a week in order to clean out its crop – the sac below the neck where the food first goes when it is swallowed. The castings are checked in the morning and removed from the mews. After these duties have been performed the hawk is left in peace to preen and relax until it is flown in the afternoon.

Correct feeding is obviously an important aspect of keeping a hawk. Birds of prey in captivity eat only raw meat, as they do in their

Left:
**The Changeable
Hawk Eagle
enjoying a bath**

Right:
**Threat display by
Savigny's Eagle Owl**

wild state. The necessity for roughage has already been mentioned. Many falconers feed a basic diet of beef and day-old chicks. The former is lean beef, purchased from a butcher, while the latter are obtained from hatcheries. Chicks are extremely valuable as a form of food for hawks. They are fed in their entirety and thus provide roughage. Falconers also feed up their birds on the quarry that they catch. This supplements the diet with a variety of natural food. A stock of hawk food is kept in a deep-freeze to maintain freshness.

Every year a hawk goes into moult. This usually starts at the end of March or April, and continues for five or six months. Thus most falconers do not fly their hawks during the summer months, preferring to 'put them down to moult' so that they bring down a fresh set of undamaged feathers. Falconers who have the necessary facilities often turn their hawks loose to moult in the mews, so that the bird can still exercise during its period of inactivity. It is possible to fly a hawk through the moult, but it requires more proficiency and care on the part of the falconer. During the moult the diet of a hawk is usually supplemented with vitamin powder, of the type given to dogs and cats, to aid feather growth. Birds which are upset during the moult will sometimes bring down new feathers which have a fault or flaw in them. These blemishes are called 'fret marks'. Similar flaws occur in new feathers when a hawk is deprived of sufficient food. These marks are termed 'hunger traces'.

When a hawk is moulting, the falconer saves the undamaged flight feathers for 'imping'. This is the process of mending a broken feather. The shaft of a feather is hollow. When a break occurs, a falconer can cut through the shaft of the broken feather, leaving a stub in the bird. An identical undamaged moulted feather is then cut to the correct length. The stub and the new feather are joined with the aid of a wooden plug, carved from bamboo or similar to fit inside the feather shaft snugly. This is covered in glue, and then slotted into the stub and the new feather. The join is squeezed shut and the freshly imped feather is treated with care until the glue has set. This process is only used for the major flight feathers on the wings and tail. Imping is unsuitable and unnecessary for smaller feathers.

Like human fingernails, a hawk's talons and beak will grow over a period of months. In the wild, birds of prey strop their beaks and wear down their feet on rocks or on the bones of their prey, but in captivity the beak and talons will often become overgrown. This excess growth must be removed, and the original shape restored with a file. This process is termed 'coping'. The bird is 'cast' – held firmly around the body with its wings folded – by an assistant, allowing the falconer both hands free to file the beak and talons back to shape. Skilful coping is an art which improves with practice.

Birds of prey are prone to picking up mites and lice. A pyrethrum-based spray is used to rid a hawk of these unwelcome little visitors. Many of the dog, cat and poultry sprays are unsafe for use on hawks, and will often prove fatal within forty-eight hours.

There are various signs which enable a falconer to tell if his hawk is healthy. A healthy hawk will have bright, round eyes. It will sit with one foot tucked up as a sign of contentment, will preen regularly, and take a lively interest in the goings on around it. Similarly there are various signs which enable a falconer to tell if his hawk is unwell, such as discoloured mutes, ill-formed castings, and 'slitty' eyes. In recent years, great advances have been made in the field of raptor medicine. There is an excellent book entitled *Veterinary Aspects of Captive Birds of Prey*, by John Cooper, M.R.C.V.S., published by The Standfast Press. It includes detailed information about diagnosis and treatment. However, most vets are inexperienced in bird of prey diseases, and consequently sensible falconers take a copy of the aforementioned book with them when they take a sick hawk to their local vet.

The aggressive head of a Golden Eagle

26

4 The Basics of Training

African Bateleur
Eagle with his crest
raised

The first stage in the training of a hawk is called 'manning'. This process involves initially persuading the hawk to sit up on the fist, and eventually accustoming it to a variety of new and different surroundings of the type that it will encounter during its life with the falconer. Getting a hawk to accept the fist as a safe perch is often a time-consuming process. The old-fashioned way of achieving this aim was to put the hawk through a process called 'waking'. This meant that the falconer would take up his freshly jessed hawk for the first time and keep it on the fist all through the day and on into the night. By nightfall, both man and bird would become tired, but the falconer would stay awake, keeping his hawk awake too. Eventually the bird would become so exhausted that, overcoming its fear of man, it would sleep on the fist. The falconer then knew that his hawk had accepted the fist as a safe perch. Nowadays, this method is only used by a few falconers in very extreme cases. The modern approach is to give the hawk an hour or two of manning at a time over a period of a few days until the hawk is reasonably steady on the fist. Some birds respond more quickly than others – it really depends upon the individual. However, there are some species which are notorious for their nervousness. The family name for these birds is 'accipiters'. These are the true hawks, the British examples of which are the Sparrowhawk and the Goshawk. These birds are therefore only suitable for experienced falconers.

As soon as the hawk will sit on the fist without bating – attempting to fly off the fist – constantly while in the confines of the mews or weathering ground, it is then taken out and about, to meet such horrors as motor vehicles, dogs, children, lawnmowers, cows, etc. This all takes a fair amount of time and a great deal of patience on the part of the falconer. Eventually, the hawk settles, and becomes more alert, removing its fixed glare from the falconer and taking a keen interest in its surroundings whilst on the fist. When the hawk no longer bates at the falconer's approach, it is ready for the next stage of training.

The next stage involves food. A hawk's food intake must be gradually reduced until it becomes hungry. This is not a cruel process. A hawk, like an athlete, must be in peak condition if it is to perform well. An overweight athlete will not run; similarly an overweight hawk will not fly. Moreover an undernourished athlete *cannot* run, and the same principle applies to a hawk. Thus the falconer must adjust his hawk's weight until it is keen enough to respond for food, being very careful not to drop its weight too low. This process is called finding the flying weight, and usually takes a week or two, although it varies considerably according to the experience of the falconer and the responsiveness of the hawk. The hawk is weighed daily, after it has cast if it has been fed casting. Whilst its weight is coming down, the falconer starts the training, and the degree of daily improvement is consequently largely (but not solely) proportional to the reduction in weight. The first step is to persuade the

Left:
**Philippine Eagle –
the second largest
eagle in the world**

Right:
**Flying free – the
Long-legged
Buzzard lands on
the fist**

hawk to eat food from the fist. From the hawk's point of view, this means that it has to take its eyes off the falconer in order to bend its head to pull at the meat. Eventually, hunger conquers nerves, and after two or so days of eating all its food from the fist, the hawk is ready to advance.

The hawk must be encouraged to jump to the fist for food. Initially this is done while the bird is tethered to its block. The aim is to get it to jump a couple of inches to take a piece of meat from the fist. The hawk normally spends quite a time leaning precariously off its block trying to snatch the meat, but after a while it plucks up courage and jumps on to the fist to take the food. If it does not, it is not fed that day, in order to ensure results the following day. When the bird is jumping the length of its leash quickly, the leash is removed and the creance is attached to the swivel. The distance the hawk is called is then increased gradually. When the hawk is responding quickly over a distance of between 50 and 100 yards, the falconer knows that he has found its flying weight, and thereafter he holds its weight steady. At this stage, the hawk is ready to be flown free. The creance and the swivel are removed and the hawk is flown completely free, with just the jesses trailing, to enable the falconer to hold the hawk when it alights on the fist.

The training of a shortwing (hawk) differs from that of a longwing (falcon). A shortwing, when it reaches the stage of flying free, is cast – propelled gently off the fist – into a tree, and then recalled to the fist. Once absolute obedience to the fist has been established, the hawk is introduced to the rabbit lure. The lure is placed in various different places until the hawk learns the importance of being alert and watchful for little furry objects that run out of bushes. The next stage – introduction to quarry – is a natural progression, as soon as the hawk is fit.

Hunting involves taking the hawk out on the fist to an area where there is some quarry about. It is usually hard work. It involves a great deal of tramping about over muddy fields searching for elusive and un-sporting rabbits, who generally sit beside their holes, diving for cover instantly a hawk appears over the horizon. The good flights at quarry, however, make all the patient (and impatient) hours of training worthwhile. Not until your first hawk, trained by you from scratch, has made its first kill can you correctly award yourself the title of falconer.

The training of longwings follows a different course, because as previously explained, long-wings take their prey in the air. The swing lure is introduced as soon as the falcon is flying a few feet to the fist, while still on the creance. The lure is swung and dropped out onto the ground a few feet in front of the falcon. Eventually she flutters down on to the ground to investigate, and saunters up to the lure to pull at the meat. Like the shortwing and the rabbit lure, the association between the shape of the lure and food quickly builds up and soon the falcon flies instantly towards the lure as soon as the falconer produces it out of his bag and starts to swing it. The bird is then flown free. The falconer starts to pull the lure out of the falcon's way. This process is called 'stooping to the lure'. Once a falcon has started stooping to the lure it becomes simply a question of building up the number of stoops. This serves a dual purpose. It builds up the falcon's fitness, and it also teaches her that she will have to persevere at quarry. Lure swinging is difficult and needs considerable practice. A good lure-swinger will time the falcon's stoops so well that it will make a falcon feel that if she just tried a little harder she would get it the next time.

Introducing or 'entering' a falcon to quarry is fairly straightforward in theory. The association between feathers and food has already been established by the lure. The falcon is slipped out of the hood upwind at quarry. Falcons can only be hunted in very open country. The reason for this is because when they are on the wing, they have a tremendous range of vision, and can see and chase a bird which is maybe several miles away. If the terrain is wooded, the falconer will

Golden Eagle assuming the 'mantling' posture adopted when on quarry

quickly lose sight of his falcon behind a bank of trees and may eventually lose her for good. Falconers are therefore restricted to hunting falcons in open areas, such as Salisbury Plain, or the Scottish grouse moors. Hawks, however, do not climb to tremendous heights and spot prey at a distance. They work close to the falconer — either directly off the fist, or out of trees while the falconer beats to flush quarry beneath his hawk. A hawk can therefore be flown in enclosed or lightly wooded countryside. Thus it is obvious that the type of bird a falconer can fly depends largely on the type of surrounding countryside.

I would like to stress that training any bird of prey is not an easy process. It involves dedication, time, facilities, and land. This chapter is in no way intended as a do-it-yourself guide to training a bird. It is simply intended to give an interested reader some idea of the theory behind training a hawk. Indeed, it is not possible to learn how to train a hawk from information contained in the pages of any book, however detailed. There can be no substitute for the advice and practical demonstration of an experienced falconer.

The author with a 'cadge' of falcons. This device enables the falconer to carry several hooded falcons at one time

5 Falconry Birds

Pallas's Sea Eagle

Choice of the right bird to suit the individual circumstances of the falconer is undoubtedly a very important step. Beginners usually expect to start with a Kestrel, but in my opinion the Common Buzzard is a far more suitable bird for a beginner, for reasons which will be explained in due course. Thereafter the choice is more difficult. Primarily, a falconer has to decide whether his area is most suitable for longwings or shortwings, the two major groups of birds of prey. Longwings are the true falcons. They have pointed wings, comparatively short tails, and dark eyes. They take their quarry in the air. Strictly speaking, a shortwing is a hawk, but the word shortwing is also used to cover a very large category including everything which is not a falcon, such as eagles, owls and vultures. Correctly, this category should be subdivided into shortwings and broadwings. Broadwing is a term used to denote the eagles, vultures and buzzards. Shortwings do not really have short wings, but appear in flight to have rounded ends to their wings. They have comparatively long tails and they usually take their prey on the ground. Their long tails aid manoeuvrability, and this is why they can be flown in wooded areas. Eagles cannot be flown in country which is too enclosed. They work best in hill country where they can use the thermals. The different species of birds normally used for falconry have varying abilities and potential, so they are best studied individually.

The Kestrel (*Falco tinnunculus*)

In falconry circles this little falcon is widely recommended as the beginner's bird, being commonly bred in captivity, and relatively easy to handle. I do not agree, however, that a kestrel should be a first bird, mainly because it takes experience to judge its correct flying weight. A kestrel is only a small bird (the females are larger than the males, as in almost every species of bird of prey). It usually only needs to lose half to one ounce to reach its flying weight. If the weight is dropped even a quarter-of-an-ounce too low, the effects can be disastrous. The beginner, therefore, is far better advised to start with a larger bird, which will give him a greater safety margin. Once accustomed to recording a bird's weight daily, and judging its performance accordingly, the beginner can try keeping a kestrel with some confidence.

Kestrels are trained in the same manner as any other longwing, but cannot usually be persuaded to hunt. This is partly because of their small size, but mainly because they show no inclination to chase quarry, being naturally lazy and lacking persistence. They quickly become 'lure-bound'. This means that they are so accustomed to the lure that they seem incapable of recognizing live quarry as food. Because kestrels lack enthusiasm at quarry when trained for falconry, they cannot strictly be described as falconry birds. However, they are extremely useful for an inexperienced

falconer to learn how to swing a lure for a falcon, and consequently are ideal as a second bird for a falconer wishing eventually to progress to larger longwings.

Buzzards (*Buteo*)

There are many different species of buzzard belonging to the family called *Buteo*. The *Buteo* family as a whole is useful to falconers. There is great variation in size and colour between the different subspecies, and similarly tremendous variation in the performance of the different types when trained for falconry, but if all the buzzards have one thing in common, it is their steadiness in the hands of the most inexperienced beginner. For this reason they are ideally suited as beginner's birds.

The Common or European Buzzard (*Buteo buteo*)

This is the native British *Buteo* used for falconry. From the beginner's point of view it has several points in its favour. Firstly, the Common Buzzard is a reasonably tough bird, which is able to withstand a certain amount of mismanagement in finding its flying weight. Indeed, it will often respond to initial efforts to fly it while still well above its correct flying weight. Secondly, a Buzzard is blessed with a relatively even temperament, and the work put in on manning is quickly rewarded. Additional points in its favour are that it is not easy to lose, being larger than a kestrel and working reasonably close to the falconer; furthermore, a falconer stands a chance of eventually being able to hunt a buzzard.

With my husband I teach falconry to students who come on courses at our falconry school. Beginners always fly a Common Buzzard, so in the past I have worked many buzzards up to and beyond the stage of flying free. Although buzzards are sometimes described as lazy, I have never encountered one which has not responded reasonably quickly to training. As these birds were a variety of ages and from varying backgrounds, I am of the opinion that an 'untrainable' Buzzard is indeed rare. I am sure that if a buzzard refuses to progress, it is normally due to a mistake on the part of the falconer, rather than to stubbornness on the part of the bird. Common Buzzards are not particularly good on quarry, but with a lot of perseverance, they can be persuaded to take rabbit, moorhen and squirrel.

The Red-tailed Buzzard (*Buteo jamaicensis*)

This is the larger American cousin to the European Buzzard. It has a high potential as a general-purpose hawk, which can be flown successfully at varied quarry, while maintaining all the other positive *Buteo* qualities rendering it suitable for a beginner. In America, therefore, the Red-tail is widely used as a beginner's bird because the American Kestrel (*Falco sparverius*) offers the same problems to a beginner as the British Kestrel. In Britain Red-tails are much more difficult to get hold of than a Common Buzzard, and consequently they are beyond the reach of the average beginner.

Red-tails are mainly successful at ground quarries, particularly rabbit, and females are quite capable of taking and holding a brown hare. Occasionally, they will fly pheasant. These they take just as the pheasant lifts off the ground.

The Ferruginous Buzzard (*Buteo regalis*)

These buzzards from western North America are slightly larger than the Red-tail. Some American naturalists feel that the Ferruginous should be reclassified as a true Eagle (*Aquila*) because they resemble an eagle in both habit and structure. In their wild state their prey includes feathered game, such as pheasant, partridge and grouse, but trained birds do not often take feathered quarry. American falconers have flown them successfully at black-tailed jack rabbits and prairie hares. The females are, in proportion to their size, tremendously powerful, and tend to be unpredictable in

Left:
A Common Buzzard landing on the fist – this is an ideal bird for a beginner

Right:
An American Red-tailed Hawk – these birds are used by beginners in America

terms of temperament. They are an ideal bird for a falconer to train if he wishes eventually to attempt to train an eagle, for through a Ferruginous he can experience something of the size and temperament of a small eagle.

The Harris' Hawk
(*Parabuteo unicinctus*)

Sometimes referred to as the Bay-winged Hawk, the Harris' Hawk is extremely responsive when used for falconry. It is often described as the ideal 'weekend falconer's' bird, for a variety of reasons. Firstly, once trained it does not need a great deal of exercise to stay fit. Secondly, its steadiness of temperament enables the falconer to pick it up, not having worked it at all during the week, take it straight out and enjoy two days of hunting. Harrises are exceptionally good-tempered and tame, and they are remarkably easy to enter at quarry. They will often soar and make a series of shallow stoops at flying game. Males will take birds as small as sparrows, as well as quail, duck, pheasant, rabbit and squirrels. Females will also take hare. The males are much quicker on the turn by virtue of their size. They have astonishing powers of acceleration and they can also wait above cover in a motion best described as hovering. Often they will kill prey in thick ground cover. The females fly in a more deliberate manner, in accordance with their size and power, but they too are capable of dramatic acceleration when in hot pursuit. On the whole they will not enter cover, but will wait for the game to be flushed. Generally speaking, the males are more stylish and versatile, whereas the females are steadier and more reliable. Harris' Hawks are sociable birds, and can be flown several at a time. It is interesting that the males will often take bigger quarry than usual when they are flown with a female. This phenomenon can probably be attributed to their gregarious behaviour when in their wild state.

A Ferruginous Buzzard

Hawks (Accipiters)

The true hawks, of the family called accipiters, are difficult birds to manage. Although they are all good hunting birds, they are exceptionally nervy and prone to throwing fits which usually prove fatal. The reason for these fits is not normally apparent, and thus they can only be generally attributed to temperament. Despite this, accipiters are widely used for falconry because of their abilities in the hunting field. They are totally unsuitable for beginners, needing a very experienced falconer to handle them.

The Sparrowhawk (*Accipiter nisus*)

In falconry terms, Sparrowhawks are delicate, tricky birds. Initially they are extremely difficult to man, and they are especially prone to throwing fits. Once trained, they will take a variety of small birds, up to the size of moorhen. They are undoubtedly one of the most difficult birds to fly and maintain for falconry purposes.

The Goshawk (*Accipiter gentilis*)

The Goshawk is the larger cousin of the Sparrowhawk. Although equally as nervy and unpredictable, the Goshawk is less delicate than the Sparrowhawk by virtue of its larger size. In falconry circles, it is widely considered to be the ultimate shortwing for hawking. Goshawks will take a vast range of quarry including rabbit, duck, pheasant, partridge, pigeon, hare and squirrel.

The Sharp-shinned Hawk
(*Accipiter striatus*)

This little hawk is found in various parts of America, Mexico and Canada. It is even smaller than the British Sparrowhawk — male sharp-shinned Hawks, or 'Sharpies', as they are called, fly at a mere $3\frac{1}{4}$oz. Their size obviously makes them extremely vulnerable to the slightest error on the part of the falconer. They have been

Left:
A Harris' Hawk –
standing with one
leg tucked up is a
sign of contentment

Right:
**A female
Sparrowhawk** –
these slender little
birds are difficult
to maintain

described as 'easily injured, difficult to handle, fearful and touchy'. However, the more experienced and persevering American falconers have had a great deal of success with them. They are normally entered at sparrows, and can be persuaded to fly a variety of small birds including meadowlarks, quail, pheasant poults and occasionally snipe. They can be very persistent and will sometimes chase for several hundred feet, culminating in a dive into cover, where, aided by their small size, they can make a kill while actually in the midst of dense ground cover.

The Cooper's Hawk
(*Accipiter cooperii*)
This is another American hawk. It is between the Sparrowhawk and the Goshawk in size. Its special qualities are its calculating attacks on clearly visible quarry, particularly quail, which it will follow into dense cover.

In most countries where falconry is practised, there appear to be near-equivalents to Sparrowhawks and Goshawks. These are worked accordingly, but are seldom seen outside their native countries.

The Falcons (Falconidae)
The falcons, or longwings, are widely used for falconry. They are generally easy to man, easy to train and get fit, but often difficult to enter at quarry.

The Peregrine (*Falco peregrinus*)
The Peregrine enjoys the worldwide reputation of being the best longwing for falconry. It is highly prized for its speed and beauty. It is normally flown in Britain in one of two different ways – for rook hawking or for game hawking. The basic difference between these two types of hawking is that rook hawks are stooped to the lure to build up fitness to chase rooks, while game hawks are never stooped to a lure, but are trained

to climb to a great height and 'wait on' – circle above the falconer – waiting for game to be flushed beneath them. They then stoop at the game, gaining tremendous speed, and strike the prey with their feet as they close on it.

Of all the forms of hawking, game hawking is the most demanding of both time and money, and consequently it is a pastime in which few falconers can indulge. In Britain the grouse season opens on 12 August – the 'Glorious Twelfth'. Falconers train both hawks and dogs on the grouse moors to have them ready for this date. Pointers are used to point game, and often spaniels are used too, to flush the quarry. The whole operation involves a great deal of organization and expertise.

The Merlin (*Falco columbarius*)
Traditionally the ladies' hawks, these little falcons are both easy and quick to train. Their affectionate disposition soon renders them very tame, and therefore, unlike most falcons, they are rarely hooded. Merlins are very small, and consequently their weight must be finely adjusted. Many falconers fly Merlins twice a day, morning and evening. Even an hour or so can make all the difference in a Merlin's weight; therefore their flying times must be very regular.

Merlins are flown mainly at larks. They are entered at the beginning of August while the young larks are making their early sorties, and the old larks are heavily in the moult. Most Merlins will usually take the first lark which is put up for them. Early success is essential because Merlins become very quickly discouraged. Later in the season, a Merlin will encounter 'ringers'. These are larks which circle or ring up very high, a feat which can only be performed by the older larks when they have almost completed the moult, and by young larks when they have become strong on the wing. Thus 'ringers' are not encountered until later on in August. The lark hawking season lasts only six weeks or so, because after this time, the larks are more than

Left:
**Hooded Peregrine
Falcon in immature
(first year) plumage**

Right:
**A jack (male)
Merlin**

capable of outflying even the best of Merlins. As they have delicate constitutions, Merlins are fed up well over the winter months.

The Hobby (*Falco subbuteo*)

Although it was the bird of the 'young gentleman' in the Middle Ages, the Hobby is rarely flown nowadays. It is extremely fast to the lure, climbing almost vertically upwards, and nearly somersaulting as it flips over to stoop at the lure. However, it is virtually impossible to persuade a Hobby to hunt small birds. Although it can easily catch almost any small bird by merit of speed, a Hobby will eat insects constantly while on the wing, thereby taking the edge off its appetite. Hobbies are relatively rare, and thus very few are flown for falconry.

The Lanner Falcon

(*Falco biarmicus*)

The Lanner is an African falcon which is very popular amongst falconers. It is an attractive falcon, slightly smaller than the Peregrine. When trained, a Lanner will put up a better display to the lure than almost any other trained falcon. In Britain it will take rook, magpie, mallard and moorhen. In their native Africa Lanners will take small game birds, including francolin and quail. The Lanner is ideal as a first 'large falcon' for a falconer to train after a kestrel.

The Lugger Falcon (*Falco jugger*)

Lugger falcons are the Indian cousins of Lanner Falcons. They are similar in size and appearance, but do not quite match the Lanner in terms of performance. Although they will fly well to the lure, they are lazy birds, and cannot usually be persuaded to take quarry other than moorhens, which are relatively easy game. However, they are, like Lanners, suitable for inexperienced falconers who need to learn the art of lure swinging.

The Saker Falcon (*Falco cherrug*)

These are large and attractive sandy-coloured falcons, which are widely used in Arabia. The Arab falconers fly them mainly at the MacQueen's Bustard, which they call 'houbara'. The equipment which the Arabic falconers use is very different from that in the Western world. Instead of falconry gloves they use sleeves or cuffs of stiff leather, called 'mangalahs', and the falcons wear jesses of brightly coloured, plaited cotton or silk. The blocks are very ornate, often worked in silver, and the top is padded with leather or cloth. The sharp spike on the end of the block enables it to be sunk into the sand.

The Arabs take a tremendous pride in their falcons, which are treated with great love and respect. The falconers themselves are very knowledgeable and skilful, particularly with the Saker Falcon, which is one of only two species in which they are interested. The Peregrine Falcon is the other species used, but only Peregrines from hot countries can be flown in Arabia, as other subspecies from cooler climates could not survive in the tremendous heat of the desert sun.

The Gyrfalcon (*Falco rusticolus*)

The Gyrfalcon is the largest, fastest and most powerful of all the falcons. It is also, arguably, the most beautiful. There are several sub-species of Gyrfalcon of varying colour phases. The best known is the white Arctic Gyr. They are flown most frequently in America. A tremendous amount of space is necessary to fly them as they range up to a mile away from the falconer when being flown to the lure. They are difficult birds to maintain in captivity, and they need a great deal of hard exercise to keep them fit.

The Prairie Falcon

(*Falco mexicanus*)

Prairie Falcons are native to America, where they are very highly thought of amongst falconers. They fly very much like a Peregrine, although they are smaller. Physically they are tough, but

A mature Lugger Falcon from India

tend to be uncertain-tempered. Males are often flown at magpie, and females take rook, crow, pheasant, duck and gull.

The Eagles

Eagles present a variety of problems to falconers, most of which are directly related to their size and power. They are heavy and awkward to handle; they are lazy; they have great powers of fasting, making it extremely difficult to find their correct flying weight; they are usually temperamental and subject to quick changes of mood. They do not make good hunting birds because, being slow off the mark, they do not take many head of quarry. When trained for falconry, they tend to be 'one-man-birds'. Thus falconers who choose to fly eagles usually do so only because they want to experience the very individual rapport that can exist between an eagle and a falconer. Eagles come in various shapes and sizes. There are very few species that are commonly trained for falconry.

The Golden Eagle
(*Aquila chrysaetos*)

Golden Eagles are very difficult to train. It takes a long time to establish a working relationship with a Golden, because they embody all the awkward characteristics of eagles previously mentioned. In addition, they are extremely hard to get fit, and they quickly go out of condition if they are not flown for a couple of days. They can take quarry up to the size of a fox. Only very experienced falconers are capable of bringing a Golden Eagle into hunting condition. Imperial Eagles (*Aquila heliaca*) are smaller than Golden Eagles and therefore more manageable.

Tawny and Steppe Eagles
(*Aquila rapax rapax* and *Aquila rapax nipalensis* or *A.r. orientalis*)

Either of these species is ideal as a 'first eagle', being of reasonably manageable size. They are not particularly good hunting birds, but they can be persuaded to take rabbit, squirrel, hare and various small fry according to their individual preferences.

Hawk Eagles

There are a few species of hawk eagle which are trained for falconry. The most popular of these is the Bonelli's Eagle (*Hieraatus fasciatus*) and its African relative, the African Hawk Eagle (*Hieraatus fasciatus spilogaster*). These are long-legged, rangy birds, with powerful feet. They are good hunting birds, being fast off the fist, and very keen after quarry. Generally, they behave more like large accipiters than eagles.

Owls

Owls are not suitable for falconry. Occasionally the large European Eagle Owls and Great Horned Owls are flown by falconers, but these are the only species which can be trained to take quarry. People are often tempted to keep owls as pets. They are in fact totally unsuitable as pets, being both messy and a great tie, as they cannot be lodged like other domestic pets in kennels or in a cattery if their owners wish to go away on holiday. From the owl's point of view, it is grossly unfair to keep a bird which is not trained for falconry and therefore cannot be given proper exercise. The only correct way to keep owls is in pairs in spacious outdoor aviaries for breeding.

Before considering taking on a hawk of any sort, it must be fully understood that when a falconer obtains a hawk, he is undertaking full responsibility for a living creature. A hawk is totally reliant on the falconer for exercise and for proper daily care and attention. Falconry cannot be learnt out of books – a beginner must be taught by an experienced falconer who will teach the practicalities by demonstration. Anyone who takes on a hawk without having had any prior experience, and without the help of a knowledgeable falconer, is extremely irresponsible, and the consequences may well be fatal for the hawk.

Nias Island Serpent Eagle – this is the smallest species of eagle in the world

Left:
Tawny Eagle just after take-off

Right:
Male Golden Eagle, in 'picture postcard' pose.

Left:
**Young Barn Owls
are very comical**

**Hampton: the
European Eagle
Owl sits
thoughtfully in the
grass**

6 Conservation and the Law

There are people who believe that falconers are the enemies of wild birds of prey. This is untrue. The majority of falconers realize that in order to perpetuate the sport, the conservation of the wild population of raptors is of the greatest importance. There is a minority of people (most of whom are dealers, rather than falconers) who bring the sport of falconry into disrepute by taking protected birds of prey illegally from the wild, but this does not mean that all falconers behave in this disgraceful fashion. It is falconers who have worked to establish captive breeding as a realistic way of conserving wild populations of birds of prey. Now falconers in several countries are reaching the time when they will be breeding sufficient numbers of hawks to satisfy their own demands. Further than this, the success of the American breed-and-release schemes involving endangered species indicates that those falconers who have expert knowledge in the field of captive breeding techniques really can make a positive contribution towards conservation. Additionally, many falconers care for injured raptors which are brought to them, releasing them when they are fit to return to the wild. This is usually done at the expense of the individual who personally meets the veterinary and other expenses involved.

In terms of Legislation, the taking of wild birds of prey in Britain is currently governed by the 1954 Protection of Birds Act. This prohibits the taking of wild birds without a licence. Licences for English and Welsh birds of prey are granted by the Department of the Environment, Tollgate House, Bristol, and for Scottish birds of prey by the Scottish Home and Health Department, St Andrew's House, Edinburgh. The successful applicant is permitted to take one eyass bird of the species applied for. To apply for a licence, the falconer must be over 18 years old, and he will not be granted more than one licence a year. A licence is also required for the import or export of a bird of prey. Generally speaking, licences are not easy to obtain.

British birds of prey can be bought and sold if they are 'ABCR' – aviary bred and close rung. It is illegal to sell any British raptor which is unrung, and it is also illegal to be in possession of a recently taken bird of prey without a licence. Currently, there are no restrictions in Britain as to who may buy an ABCR bird of prey. It is left to the discretion of the person offering the bird for sale, and thus, all too often, birds of prey end up with unsuitable and ignorant people.

The Wildlife and Countryside Bill is, at the time of writing, before Parliament. This contains certain proposals concerning the keeping of birds of prey in Britain. If these proposals are implemented into law, a system of registration will be introduced for all diurnal captive birds of prey. This will mean that every legal captive raptor will have a band put round its leg, and the bird will be registered to its keeper. If the bird is sold or passed on, the authorities must be notified and the registration transferred to the new keeper. It is hoped that this will go some way towards discouraging people from taking birds of prey illegally from the wild, as such a bird will not be registered, and will consequently not only be illegal but also valueless. Information regarding the laws in Britain relating to birds of prey at any time should be obtained from the Department of the Environment, in Bristol.

In America the laws concerned with falconry vary from state to state. The Bureau of Sport, Fisheries and Wildlife prescribes the federal laws concerned with falconry. The individual state laws cannot be less restrictive than these federal

A fledgeling Kestrel bred in captivity

A wild baby Tawny Owl. All birds of prey are protected by law – please leave them alone

laws. This means that falconry is illegal in some states because the administrative cost of conforming to the federal requirements is too high. In states where falconry is legal, falconers must have a permit to practise falconry. These permits are issued by the Department of Wildlife and Fisheries in the state concerned. Most states which practise falconry have a club or society for falconers within that state. All of these clubs are affiliated to the North American Falconers' Association, which is the major falconry organization in America.

Useful Addresses

Clubs and societies
The British Falconers' Club,
c/o P T Fields,
3 Orchard Lane,
Longton,
Preston,
Lancashire

The Welsh Hawking Club,
c/o Anne Shuttleworth,
21, North Close,
Blackfordby,
Burton-on-Trent,
Staffordshire

Northern England Falconry Club,
c/o B Thelwell,
2, Fourlands Drive,
Lolle,
Bradford,
Yorkshire

North American Falconers' Association
James W Grier,
Rt 1 Hawley,
Minnesota 56549
USA

Falconry courses
Stephen and Emma Ford
The British School of Falconry
Stelling Minnis
Canterbury
Kent

Falconry courses available at beginners' and advanced level. All aspects of falconry covered.

Places to visit
The Bird of Prey Conservation & Falconry Centre,
Newent,
Gloucestershire

The Welsh Hawking Centre,
Weycock Road,
Barry,
S. Glamorgan

The Hawk Conservancy,
Weyhill,
Andover,
Hampshire

Equipment suppliers
Robin Haigh,
Abbey Bridge Farm House,
Colonel's Lane,
Chertsey
Surrey

Martin Jones,
The Lodge,
Huntley,
Gloucestershire

John Cox,
The Servant's Cottage,
White Hall,
Undy,
Gwent

Information regarding the laws concerning birds of prey
The Department of the Environment,
Tollgate House,
Bristol

The Royal Society for the Protection of Birds,
The Lodge,
Sandy,
Bedfordshire

The Scottish Home and Health Department
St Andrew's House,
Edinburgh

Glossary

ABCR Aviary bred, close rung. When a bird is bred in captivity a metal ring is placed around its leg when it is a matter of days old. The bird's leg then grows to fit the ring, proving that the bird was in captivity as a baby, rather than stolen from the wild.

Bate To attempt to fly off the fist or perch when held or tied, in fright or at the lure or quarry.

Bewit Short thin strap of leather by which the bells are fastened to the legs.

Block perch A truncated cone or cylindrical piece of wood, having a ring on it for the attachment of the leash, and placed out of doors, whereon the hawk is set to 'weather'.

Bow perch A semi-circular perch with a padded top, used for hawks out of doors.

Cast (1) To impel gently a hawk forward off the fist to get it airborne.

Cast (2) The act of disgorging a pellet of the undigested parts of a meal – fur, feather etc.

Cast (3) To hold the hawk between the hands for imping, coping etc.

Casting The pellet of feathers and fur disgorged by a hawk after completing the process of digestion.

Cope To file the beak.

Creance A light line attached to the swivel of a partly trained hawk before she is allowed to fly loose.

Enter To give a hawk its first flight at quarry.

Eyass A nestling or young hawk taken from the nest.

Furniture The falconer's equipment.

Hawk Strictly speaking, a true accipiter, but generally a term used to refer to any bird of prey flown for falconry.

Imp To mend a broken feather.

Jesses The narrow strips of leather fastened round a hawk's legs to hold her by.

Leash A long narrow thong or strip of nylon with a falconry button at one end, used to tether a hawk to her perch.

Longwing A term used to cover all falcons, who have long pointed wings and dark eyes.

Lure An imitation bird or animal used to entice the hawk back in flight.

Mews The building or room where hawks are kept. Also the place in which they are put away to moult.

Mutes The droppings or excrement of hawks.

Quarry The game at which a bird is flown.

Ring perch A perch on which the hawk sits on top of a padded circle, which in turn is attached to a stand.

Screen perch An indoor perch for a hawk, which is considered unsafe by good falconers.

Shortwing Term used to cover eagles, hawks, and buzzards, who have rounded ends to their wings when seen silhouetted in flight.

Swivel Two rings, connected in a figure of eight fashion with a bolt or rivet. Used to connect the jesses and the leash when a hawk is held or tied on the perch, to prevent them from becoming twisted.

Tiercel The male Peregrine, from the French 'tierce' meaning third, and implying a third less in size than the female. This term is often incorrectly used to cover any male bird of prey.

Wait on To circle round high up over the falconer, waiting for him to flush the quarry or throw out the lure.

Weather To place the hawk on her block in the open air during the day.

Weathering A shelter in which a hawk can be put in the open air.

Weathering ground The area where the hawks are kept on blocks through the day.

Index

Italics indicate pages on which illustrations appear